SUPER-EASY
ORiGAMi

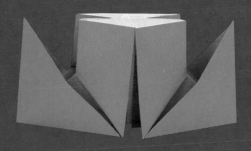

SUPER-EASY
ORIGAMI

Duy Nguyen

Sterling Publishing Co., Inc.
New York

Design by Rose Sheifer
Edited by Claire Bazinet

Library of Congress Cataloging-in-Publication Data

Nguyen, Duy, 1960-
    Super-easy origami / Duy Nguyen.
        p. cm.
    Includes index.
    ISBN 1-4027-2288-5
    1. Origami. I. Title.
TT870.N48819 2005
736'.982--dc22

                                        2005016357

10 9 8 7 6 5 4 3 2

Published by Sterling Publishing Co., Inc.
387 Park Avenue South, New York, NY 10016
© 2005 by Duy Nguyen
Distributed in Canada by Sterling Publishing
C/o Canadian Manda Group, 165 Dufferin Street
Toronto, Ontario, Canada M6K 3H6
Distributed in Great Britain and Europe by Chris Lloyd at Orca Book
Services, Stanley House, Fleets Lane, Poole BH15 3AJ, England
Distributed in Australia by Capricorn Link (Australia) Pty. Ltd.
P.O. Box 704, Windsor, NSW 2756, Australia

Sterling ISBN 1-4027-2288-5

For information about custom editions, special sales, premium and
corporate purchases, please contact Sterling Special Sales
Department at 800-805-5489 or specialsales@sterlingpub.com.

Long ago, in a city far away called Saigon, a friend let me look at a book he had.
It showed how to make things by folding paper. I was seven years old, and I learned
quickly because it was fun to do. Now I write books on folding paper.
I hope this book brings you much fun, too.

Duy Nguyen

Origami books by Duy Nguyen

Creepy Crawly Animal Origami
Dinosaur Origami
Fantasy Origami
Jungle Animal Origami
Origami Holidays
Origami Myths and Legends
Origami on the Move
Origami USA
Origami with Dollar Bills
Super-Easy Origami
Under the Sea Origami

Contents

Projects

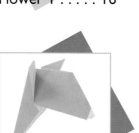

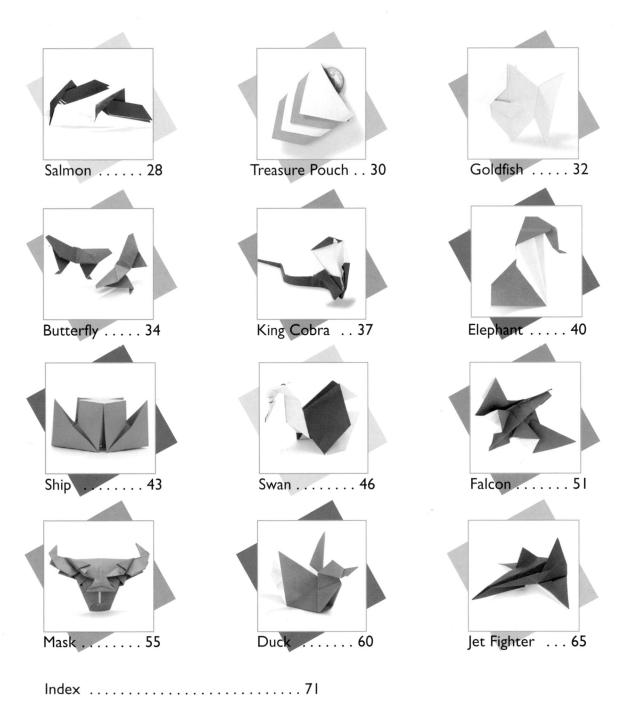

Introduction

Have you ever seen someone take a simple square of paper and fold it into strange and wonderful shapes? Folding paper like that is called Origami, and you can do it, too. It will take some practice. But once you know your valley fold from your mountain fold, and can follow a few other simple directions, you are on your way to making those strange and wonderful shapes on your own…as many as you like!

Here are step-by-step directions for making a puppy, two flowers, a goldfish, a treasure pouch, and more. There's some colorful origami paper here, too. But don't take it out yet! You are sure to make a lot of folding mistakes while you are learning. So don't use the special origami paper for practice. Cut some large squares from sheets of plain white or colored paper to practice on (see page 70). Then, when you are ready, get out the bright-colored origami paper, and go to it!

Origami Paper

Origami is folded using a special thin paper. It comes in all colors and in different size squares—usually 6 or 8 inches (about 15 or 20 cm). Here, we have supplied 40 6-inch sheets: 5 each of 8 different colors, specially printed for the projects in this book.

When choosing origami paper:

1 Look for paper that folds well and doesn't tear easily.

2 If colored paper is too heavy or thick, the color might "break" at the fold.

3 Some papers stretch, so are not good for doing origami.

4 Try out new paper by folding some scraps.

How to Fold Origami

All these projects begin with a square. Fold the paper one step at a time, following the instruction and the picture. As you make the fold for one step, look at the picture for the next step. That's what it **should** look like after you make the fold. As you fold the paper, make sure the edges of the paper line up. When you make folds at the corners, they should come to nice points. Do your origami on a clean, flat surface. Press down and run your finger, or a fingernail, down the length of the fold to press it in neatly.

Fold Lines and Symbols

These fold lines and marks will guide you:

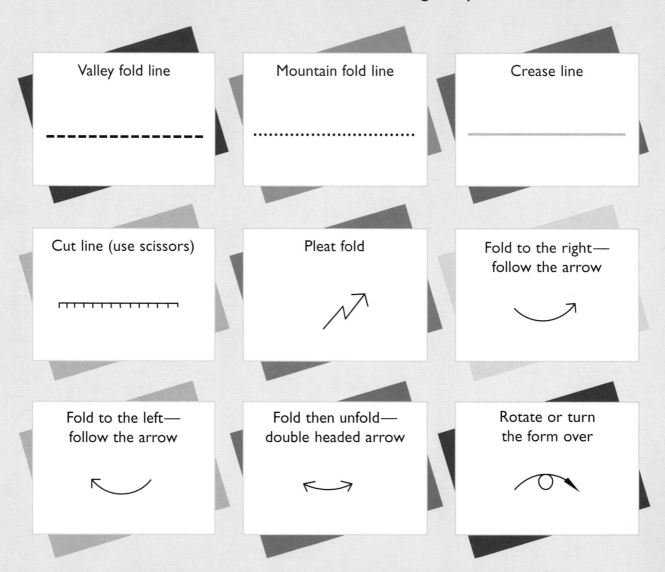

Valley fold line

Mountain fold line

Crease line

Cut line (use scissors)

Pleat fold

Fold to the right—
follow the arrow

Fold to the left—
follow the arrow

Fold then unfold—
double headed arrow

Rotate or turn
the form over

The Basic Folds

VALLEY FOLD

1. Fold the paper forward (towards you). Fold on the **dashed** line. Follow the arrow.

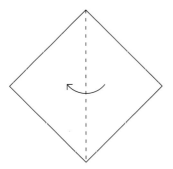

2. You've made a Valley Fold.

MOUNTAIN FOLD

1. Fold the paper backwards (away from you). Make the fold on the **dotted** line.

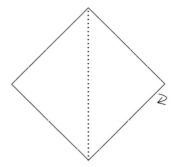

2. You've made a Mountain Fold.

Tip

To remember which line is Valley and which is Mountain, think of the line of dashes as a stream running down a valley, and the line of dots as the mountain peaks sticking up.

KITE FOLD

1. Valley fold a square of paper from corner to corner.

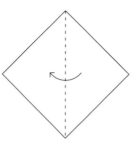

2. Unfold the paper to make a crease in the center.

3. Valley fold one side on the dashed line. Line up the paper against the center crease.

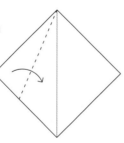

4. Valley fold the other side in, too.

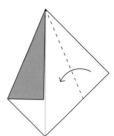

5. This is a Kite Fold.

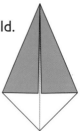

Practice with the Kite Fold

Valley fold a kite form like this:

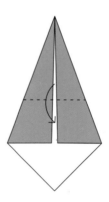

Fold it towards you on the dashed line.

Mountain fold a kite form like this:

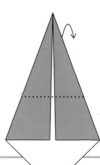

Fold it away from you on the dotted line.

INSIDE REVERSE FOLD

1. Start with a kite fold. Valley fold it in half on the dashed line.

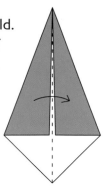

2. Pull the top point to the right and make mountain folds front and back on the dotted line.

3. It's an Inside Reverse Fold.

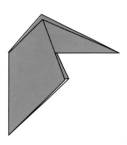

OUTSIDE REVERSE FOLD

1. Start with a kite fold. Valley fold it in half on the dashed line.

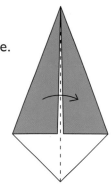

2. Pull the top point so it turns inside out. Make valley folds front and back on the dashed line.

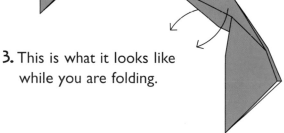

3. This is what it looks like while you are folding.

4. It's an Outside Reverse Fold.

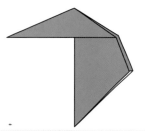

1. Start with a kite fold. Valley fold it on the dashed line.

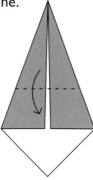

2. Now valley fold back.

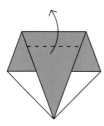

3. It's a Pleat Fold

TIP

To make a clean fold, position the paper so that the fold line will lie exactly where you want it. Then, press with your thumb or fingernail to make a nice smooth crease on the fold line.

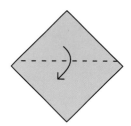

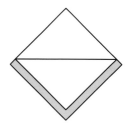

TIP

Make sure that edges line up and that tips come to a clean point when they are supposed to.

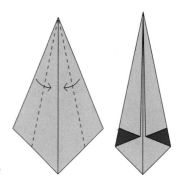

NOTE: All the projects in this book start with a regular square.

PROJECTS

FLOWER 1

Flowers come in many colors. Let's make this red one.

1 Valley fold the paper square in half on the dashed line. You are folding it diagonally, which means from corner to corner. Now unfold it. There is a crease down the middle.

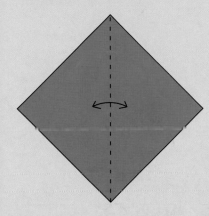

2 Valley fold both sides against the crease (look at the next step).

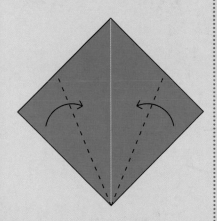

3 Valley fold both corners towards the outside.

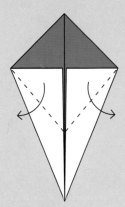

4 On the dashed line, valley fold the form in half.

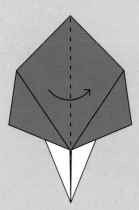

5 Make a valley fold on the dashed line, then loosen the folds.

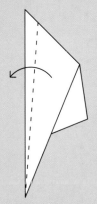

6 You've made your first Flower! Good work! Now, what can you use for a stem? How about a straw or a pipecleaner?

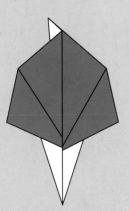

PUPPY

It's so easy to make this adorable puppy.
You can make him a friend, too.

1 Valley fold the paper from corner to corner, diagonally.

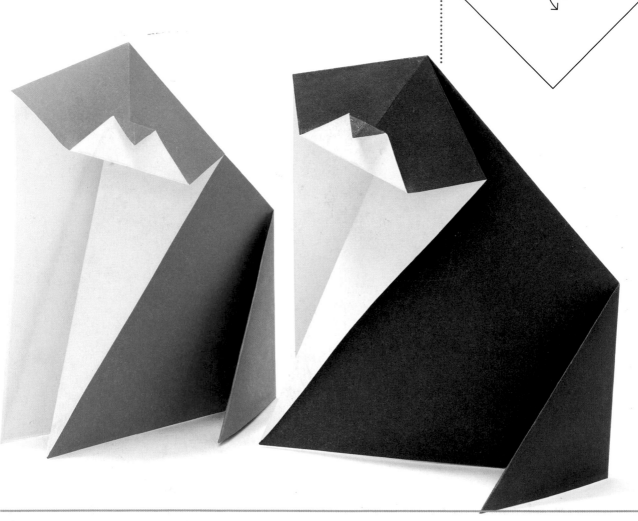

2 Make an inside reverse fold on the dotted line. (Look at the directions on page 13, and the "tip" on this page.)

TiP

Here's a way to make an inside or outside reverse fold easier to do. First, valley fold and then mountain fold the paper on the line and unfold it. Then, turn the creased folds on each side into mountain or valley folds. An inside reverse fold has mountain folds on both sides. An outside reverse fold has valley folds on both sides.

3 Valley fold the top layer of paper on the dashed line.

4 Make a valley fold upward on the dashed line.

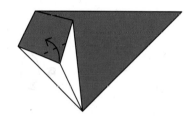

5 Valley fold the tip, to make the puppy's nose.

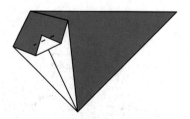

6 Valley fold the section on the right.

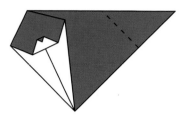

7 Turn the puppy to sit upright.

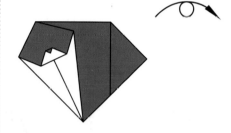

8 Here is the Puppy. Color nose and make eyes with markers.

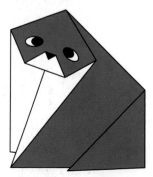

CAT

This cat is yellow, but you can make yours any color you wish.

1 Valley fold the square in half to crease, then unfold.

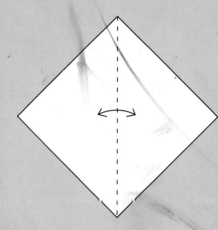

2 Valley fold the sides inward to the crease.

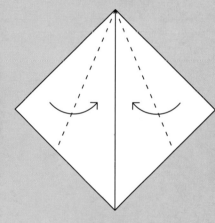

3 It's a Kite Fold! Now make a mountain fold.

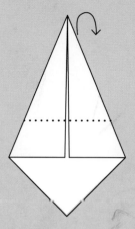

4 Valley fold the corners on the dashed line.

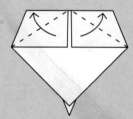

5 Valley fold the corner upward.

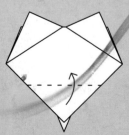

6 Valley fold the tip downward.

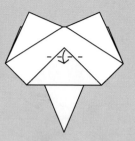

7 Here's Ginger the Cat! For these eyes, draw circles and color them in.

DOG

You can have your own dog in only eight easy steps!

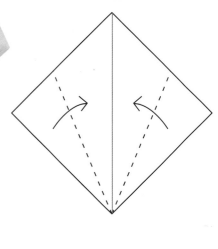

1 Valley fold the square in half to crease, then unfold.

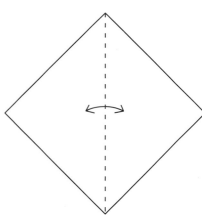

2 Valley fold the sides inward to the crease.

3 It's an upside down Kite! Now mountain fold the top.

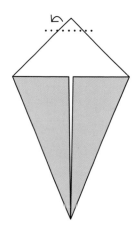

4 Make valley folds on the dashed lines.

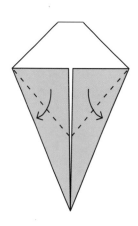

5 Mountain fold the form in half.

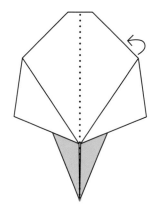

6 Valley fold on the dashed line, then turn it into an outside reverse fold.

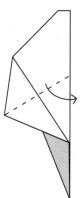

7 Valley folds on both sides to make the ears.

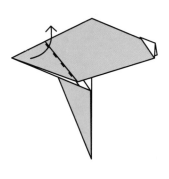

8 Great! You've made Pepper the Dog.

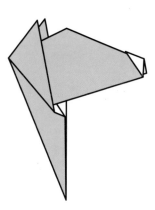

BULL

You don't need to be a matador to make this bull. Give it a shot!

1 Valley fold the square in half.

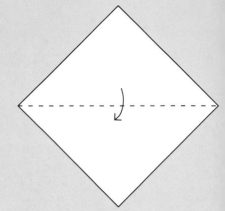

2 Mountain fold the form backwards on the dotted line.

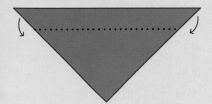

3 Make valley folds on the dashed lines (see next step).

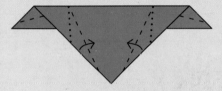

4 When it looks like this, squash the folds flat.

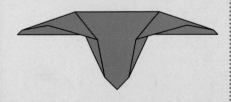

5 Valley fold each side to make the bull's horns, and valley the nose, too.

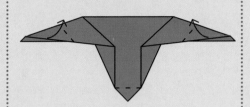

～ Tip ～

To move a fold just a little and make it stay there, squash it! It's called a squash fold. When a squash fold is on the inside, the lines don't show. When it is on the outside, you can see and follow the mountain and valley lines.

6 Mountain fold the bull in half on the dotted line and unfold.

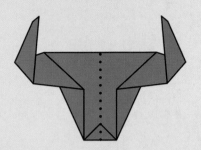

7 Look out! Here comes your Bull!

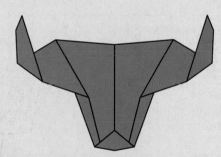

FLOWER 2

Here's another flower! Make more and you'll soon have a garden.

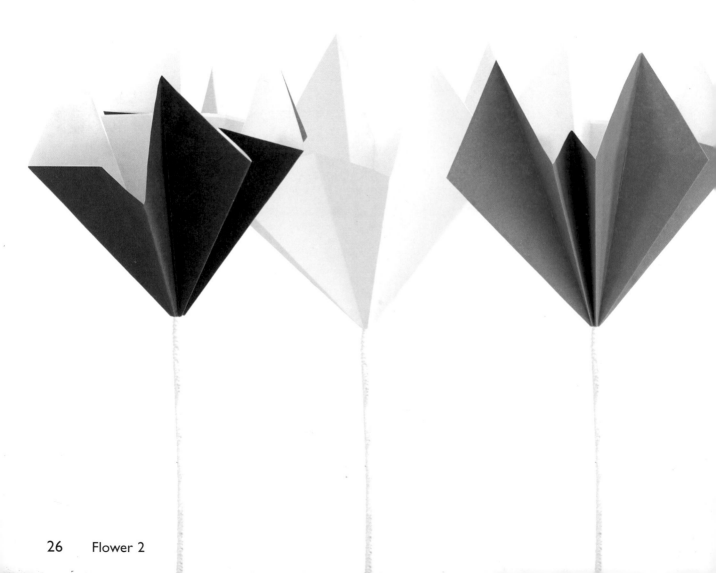

1 Valley fold the square in half.

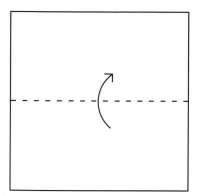

2 Valley fold the paper again on the dashed line, and unfold.

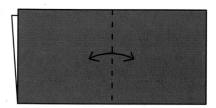

3 Valley fold and unfold again.

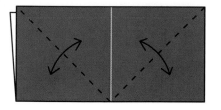

4 Using the creases, make inside reverse folds on both sides. The folds on both sides will be mountain folds.

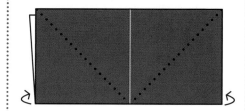

5 Make inside reverse folds again.

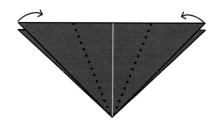

6 Turn the form over.

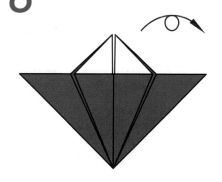

7 Make two inside reverse folds on this side.

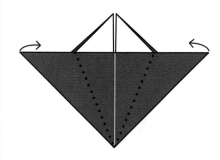

8 Now open up the folds a little.

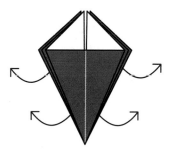

9 What a lovely Flower you've made!

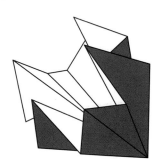

Salmon

Salmon have to jump like this over rocks when they swim upstream.

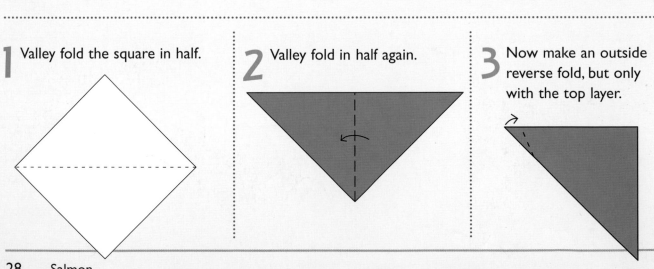

1 Valley fold the square in half.

2 Valley fold in half again.

3 Now make an outside reverse fold, but only with the top layer.

4 Mountain fold on the dotted line.

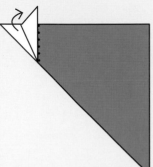

5 Valley fold both layers together.

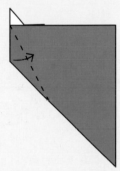

6 Mountain fold backwards, in the direction of the arrow.

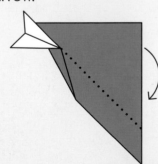

7 Turn the form over and rotate.

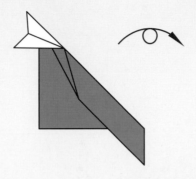

8 Following the arrow, pull the top layer downward, but just a little bit. Squash the fold flat.

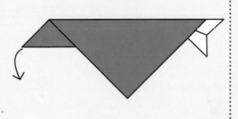

9 Valley fold on the dashed line.

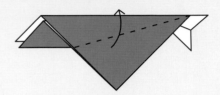

10 Now mountain fold on the dotted line.

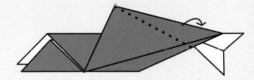

11 Look! It's a Salmon jumping! Let's make another.

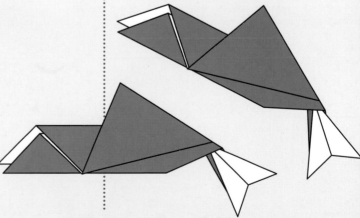

TREASURE POUCH

It's great to have something to hold tiny treasures. How about a pouch?

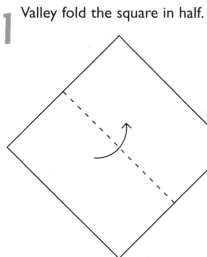

1 Valley fold the square in half.

2 Valley fold the paper in half again.

3 Now, on the dashed line, valley fold only the top layer downward.

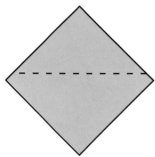

4 Is there a colored stripe at the bottom? Okay, next valley fold to leave a white stripe.

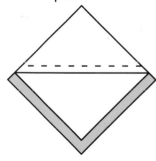

5 And valley fold again for another colored stripe.

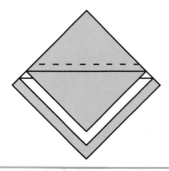

6 Mountain fold both sides to the back.

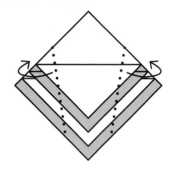

7 Mountain fold the top flap to the back.

8 Pull front and back layers apart.

9 Yes, that's good. The pouch is open.

10 Your Treasure Pouch is a real keeper!

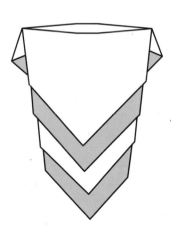

GOLDFISH

Don't make just one goldfish. Draw a fishbowl big enough to hold two or three.

1 Valley fold a square in half diagonally.

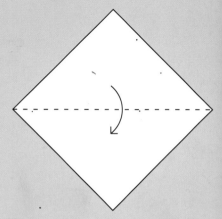

2 Next make two valley folds on the dashed lines.

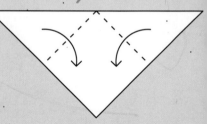

3 Valley fold the two flaps upward.

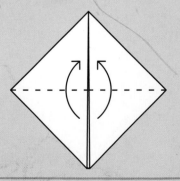

4 Then valley fold each side.

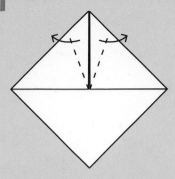

5 Now valley fold only one layer of paper upward.

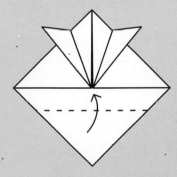

6 Valley fold that same layer upward on the dashed line.

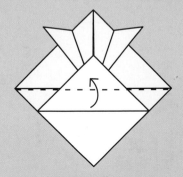

7 With your scissors, cut through the other layers as shown by the cutlines. Careful, don't cut too far!

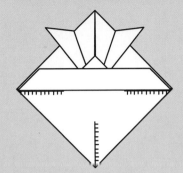

8 Mountain fold the lower flap backward.

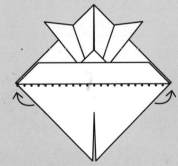

9 Pull open the front and back sections (see next step).

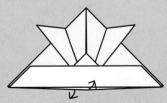

10 This is how it looks while you are pulling. Keep pulling until...

11 ...it looks like this. Then valley fold the tail fins on both front and back.

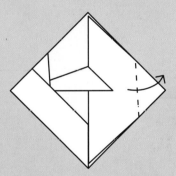

12 You've made a Goldfish! Be sure to keep the cat away from it!

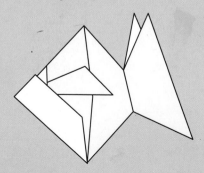

BUTTERFLY

It's fun to make lots of colorful butterflies.

1 Valley fold the square paper in half.

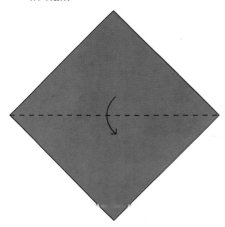

2 Valley fold to make a crease, then unfold.

3 Valley fold both layers upward together.

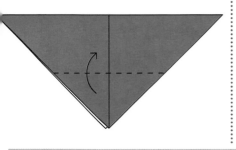

4 Now valley fold both layers, so the point is a little past the bottom edge (see next step).

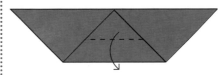

5 Mountain fold the tip backward.

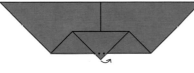

6 Valley fold the two sides on the dashed lines. Start each fold at the center crease.

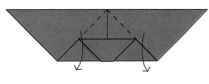

7 Valley fold the top downward.

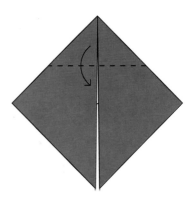

8 Mountain fold both sides backward, on the dotted line.

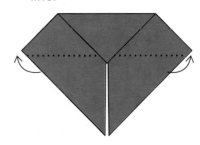

9 Turn the form over to work on the other side.

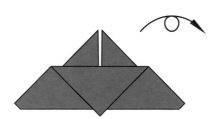

10 Pull the two sides outward a little (see next step) and squash fold.

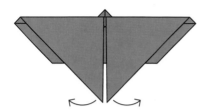

11 Valley fold the tips of the wings, and the top point.

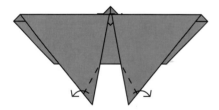

12 Bring the butterfly to life. Valley fold it in half, then unfold.

13 What a lovely Butterfly you've made!

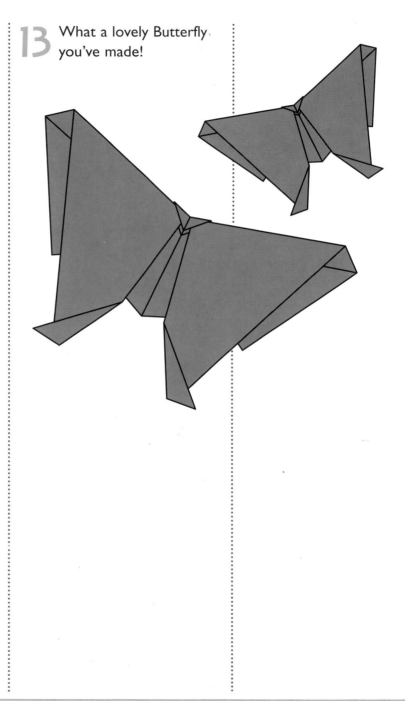

KING COBRA

You don't have to worry about getting too close to this cobra.

Tip

Add color to white paper with high-lighter, crayon, or paint. Or set your computer's printer to print out solid or patterned color paper for use in origami. You can even make two-sided color paper for special projects, like this King Cobra!

1 Start with a square. Make a valley fold on the dashed line, then unfold it.

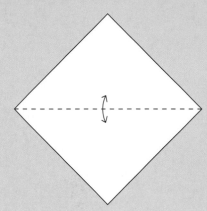

2 Make a valley fold on each of the dashed lines.

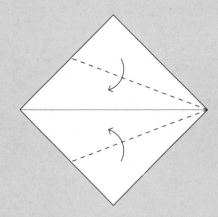

3 Now make two more valley folds.

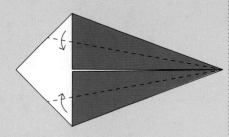

4 And two more valley folds.

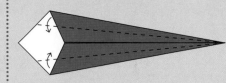

5 Now valley fold the form in half, on the dotted line.

6 Valley fold to crease, then turn it into an outside reverse fold.

7 Let's take a closer look.

8 Again, valley fold and turn it into an outside reverse fold.

9 Make another outside reverse fold right at the tip.

10 This is how it looks. Now let's do the body.

11 On the right side of the cobra, make a mountain fold.

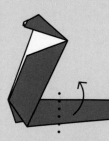

12 Turning to the cobra's left side, make another mountain fold.

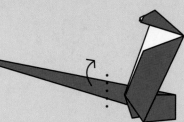

13 Go back to the right side and make another mountain fold.

14 On the dashed line, valley fold both sides to make the cobra's hood. Then shape the sharp folds of the snake's body into curves, so it looks more natural.

15 Your King Cobra is ready to stand guard at your bedside while you sleep.

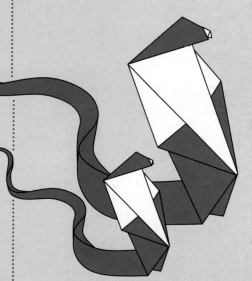

ELEPHANT

How would you like your own elephant?
Let's get started.

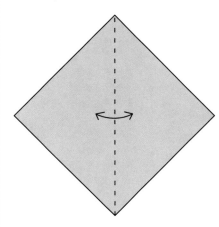

1 Valley fold on the dashed line, then unfold.

2 Make these two valley folds.

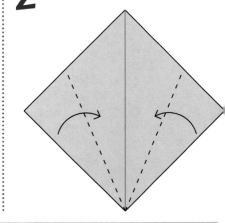

3 Now these two valley folds.

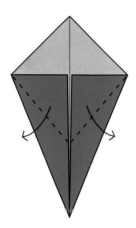

4 Valley fold the form in half.

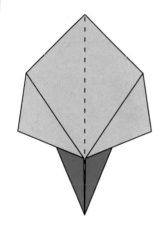

5 Rotate the form.

6 Make an inside reverse fold on the dotted line.

7 Now make an outside reverse fold on the dashed line.

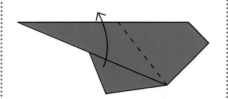

8 And another outside reverse fold.

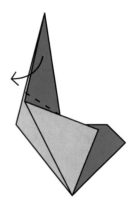

9 Rotate the form.

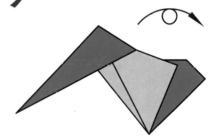

10 Make an inside reverse fold on the dotted line to form the elephant's trunk.

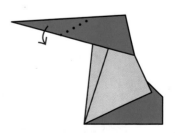

11 And another inside reverse fold.

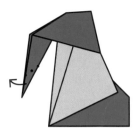

12 And another inside reverse fold to finish off the elephant's trunk.

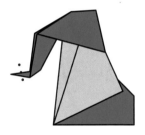

13 Now valley fold both sides and unfold, to make the ears flap.

14 Here's your Elephant—and it's sitting up! What a great trick you made it do!

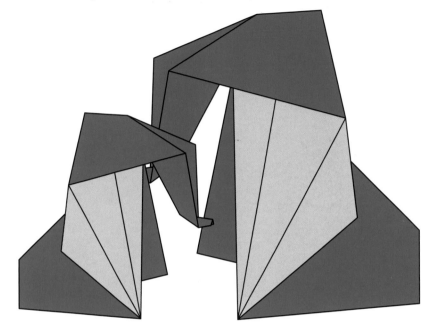

SHIP

Here you'll learn how to build your own ship.

1 Valley fold the square diagonally, and unfold it.

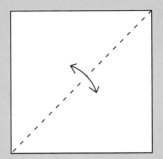

2 Valley fold to the other two corners, and unfold again.

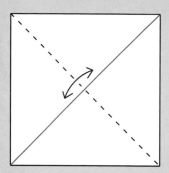

3 Valley fold the four corners inward to the center, where the creases cross.

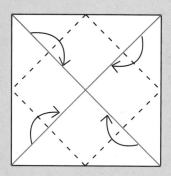

4 Turn the form over.

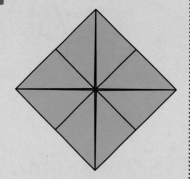

5 Valley fold the four corners inward again.

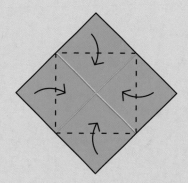

6 Turn the form over.

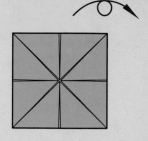

7 Valley fold the four corners inward again.

8 The square is very small now, so let's take a closer look.

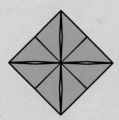

9 Pull open two of the corners and flatten the folds.

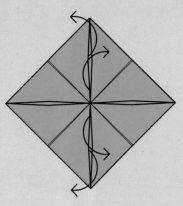

10 This is how it looks as you are pulling it open.

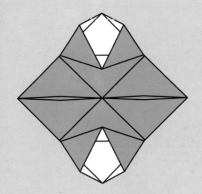

11 Now, pull the other two corners apart as shown, letting the form fold down the middle.

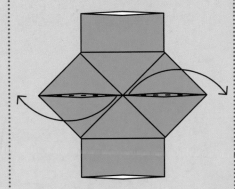

12 This is how it looks now as you pull and fold.

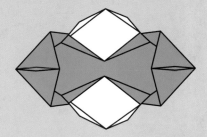

13 Turn the ship to the side.

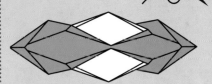

14 The Ship is finished! Who wants to go?

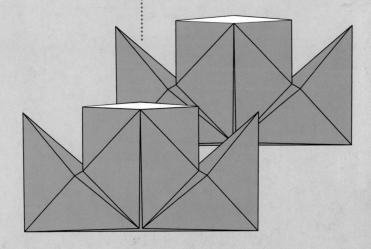

Swan

Give this lovely swan a place to swim.
A lake made of blue paper would be
do nicely.

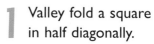
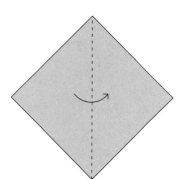

2 Valley fold the top layer.
Line up the paper with
the left edge.

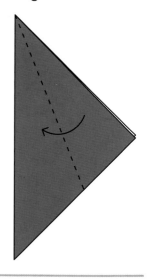

3 Turn the form over.

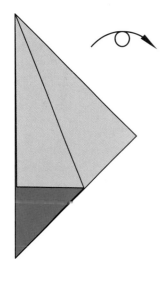

5 Unfold the top layer in the direction of the arrow.

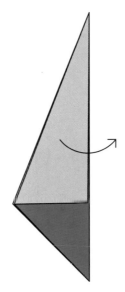

7 Mountain fold the lower half upward.

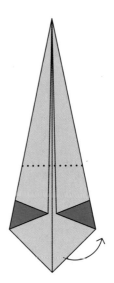

4 Valley fold the top layer, to line up with the right edge.

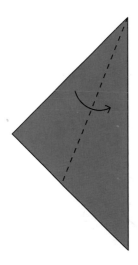

6 Valley fold each side to the center crease.

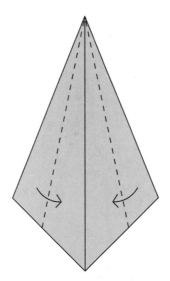

8 Turn the form around.

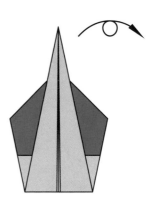

9 Valley fold on the dashed line as shown by the arrow

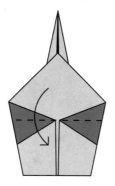

10 Mountain fold the form in half.

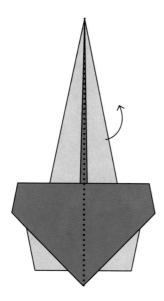

11 Turn the form to the left.

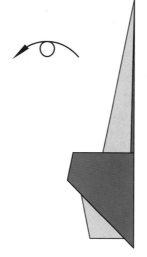

12 Pull the top layer as shown by the arrows, and squash fold the sides.

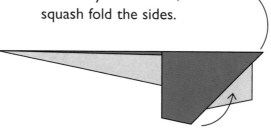

13 Make an inside reverse fold.

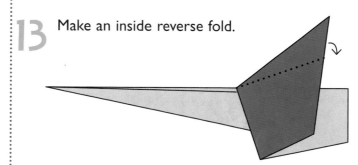

14 Mountain fold the top layer on the dotted line.

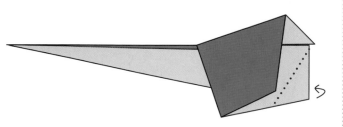

15 Valley fold the bottom layer.

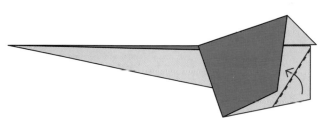

16 Tuck the flap between the center layers.

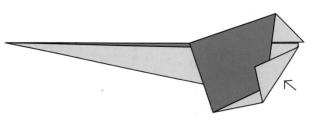

17 Make an outside reverse fold.

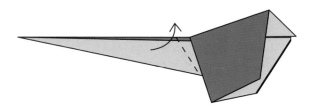

18 Make another outside reverse fold on the neck.

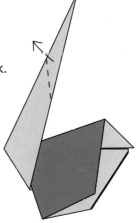

19 Make an inside reverse fold for the head.

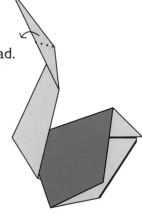

20 Let's take a closer look at these steps.

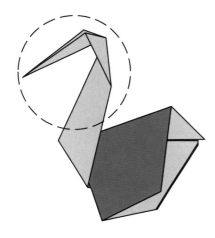

21 Valley fold the head so it is flat.

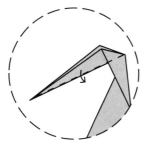

22 Make a pleat fold.

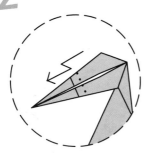

23 Valley fold the head down the middle.

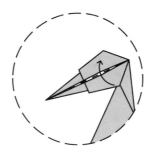

24 Pull the pleat fold slightly, and squash the fold.

25 Now the swan has a bill. We could color it yellow.

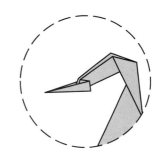

26 And you've made a Swan! You could make a lot of swans, but then you'd need a larger pond!

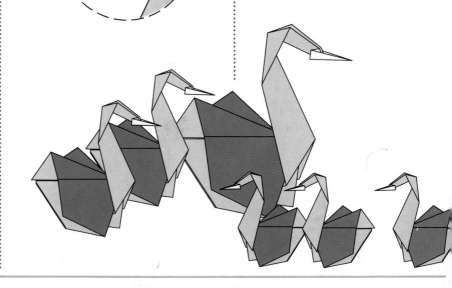

FALCON

This falcon may take quite a few steps, but you'll be creating a beautiful bird.

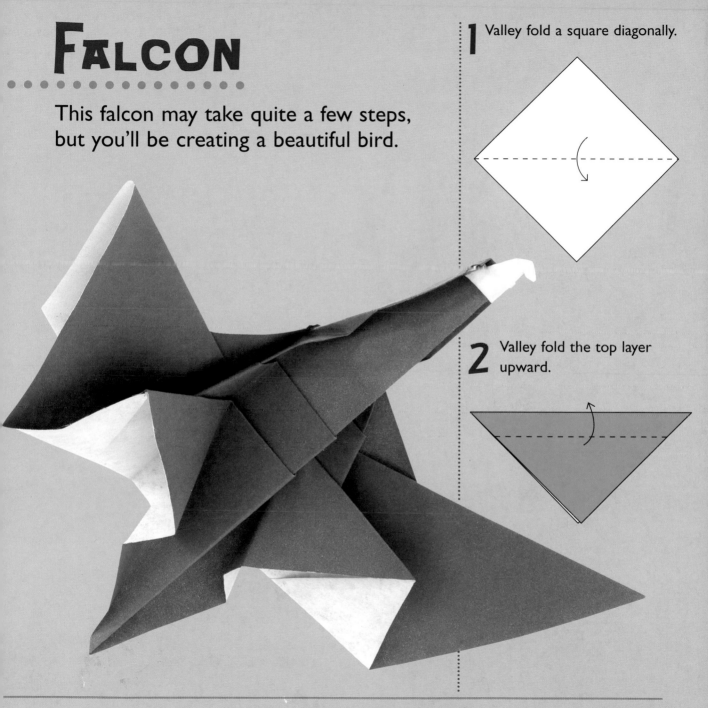

1 Valley fold a square diagonally.

2 Valley fold the top layer upward.

3 Then valley fold and unfold to crease.

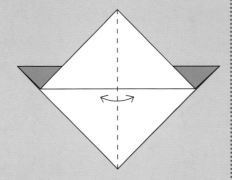

4 Valley fold the right side against the center crease.

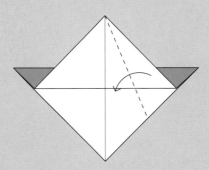

5 Valley fold back again on the dashed line.

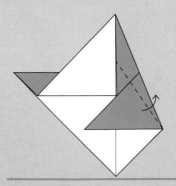

6 Now do the same on the left side. Valley fold to the center crease…

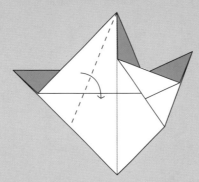

7 …and then valley fold back toward the left.

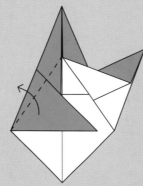

8 Turn the form over.

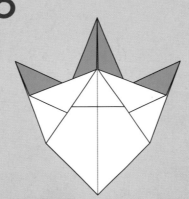

9 Make a valley fold across the form as shown.

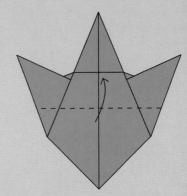

10 Now valley fold it back on the dashed line.

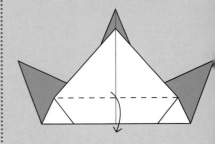

11 Make a beak on the falcon with a pleat fold (valley and mountain folds).

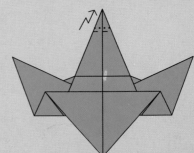

12 Mountain fold the form in half as shown by the arrow.

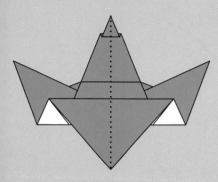

13 Rotate the falcon to the left (wings on top).

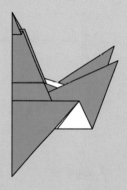

14 Let's take a closer look.

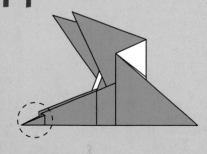

15 On the beak, make an outside reverse fold. Fold it at an angle, as shown by the dashed line.

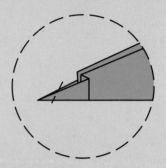

16 This is how it looks; now let's finish the body.

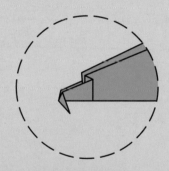

17 Valley fold the front section down the length of the body.

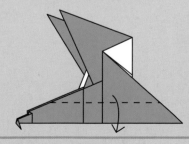

18 Mountain fold the other side of the body to match.

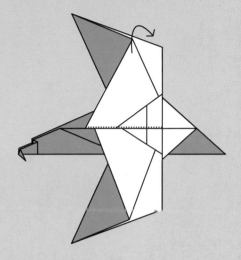

19 Now let's shape the head. Valley fold the front side.

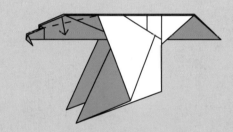

20 Mountain fold the back side.

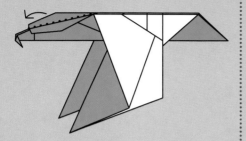

23 Balance the wings out to the sides.

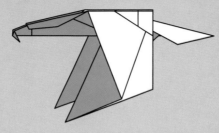

21 Now, the tail. Valley fold the front side.

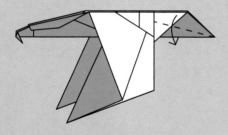

24 Your Falcon wants to fly! Attach a string and hang it up high.

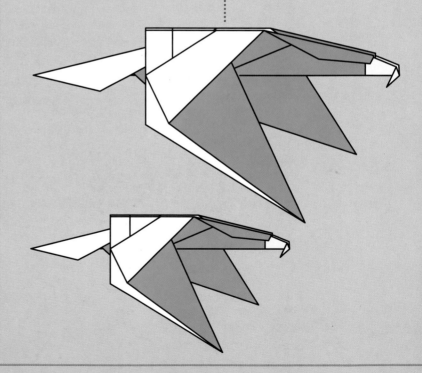

22 Mountain fold the back side.

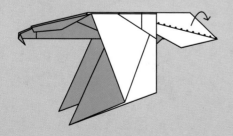

MASK

Do you like to make faces?
Here's a fun paper mask to fold.

1 Valley fold a square in half diagonally.

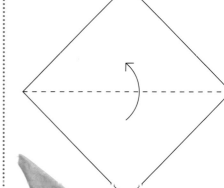

2 Valley fold both sides upward.

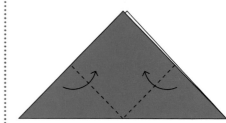

3 Now valley fold the two flaps downward.

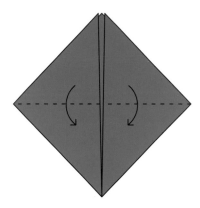

4 Then valley fold them upward again.

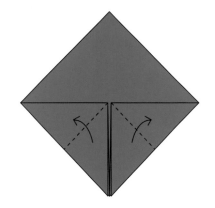

5 Make two inside reverse folds.

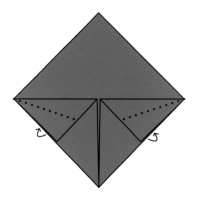

6 Mountain fold the side sections on the dotted lines.

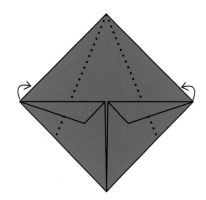

7 Valley fold each side on the dashed lines.

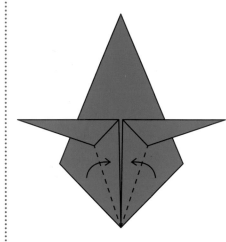

8 Valley fold the corners downward.

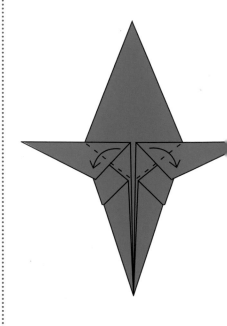

9 Now, valley fold them upward.

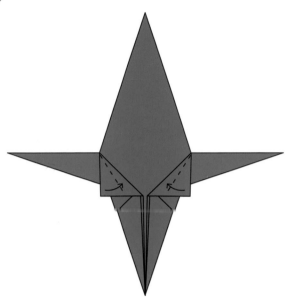

11 Make inside reverse folds for the mask's horns.

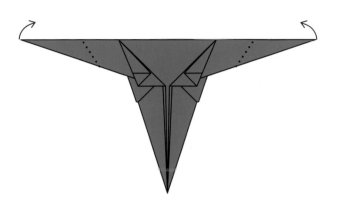

10 Mountain fold the top on the dotted line.

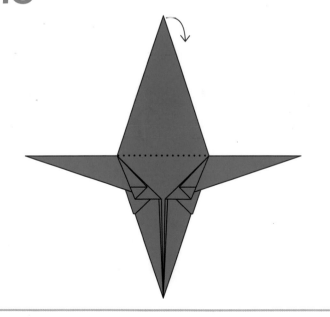

12 Make a pleat fold for the face.

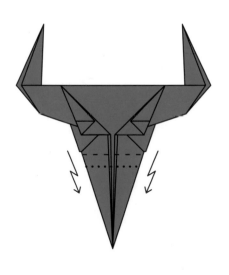

13 Now valley fold the nose upward.

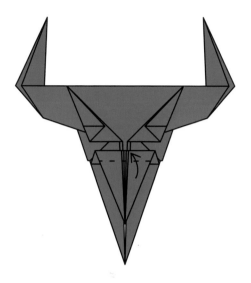

14 Valley fold the point at the bottom.

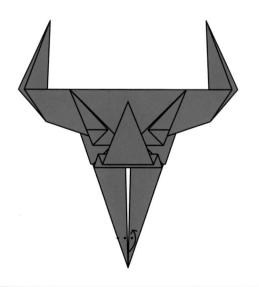

15 Valley fold the lower section upward.

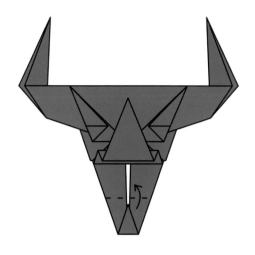

16 Mountain fold the mask in half.

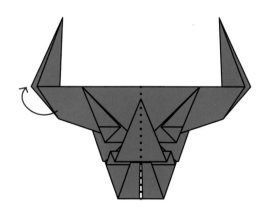

17 Pull the nose and mouth sections open, and squash fold them into position.

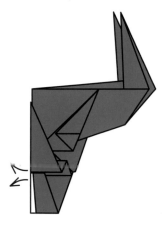

18 Now open the fold to face you.

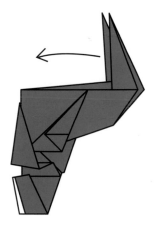

19 That's a scary Mask! Hang it on your door for privacy.

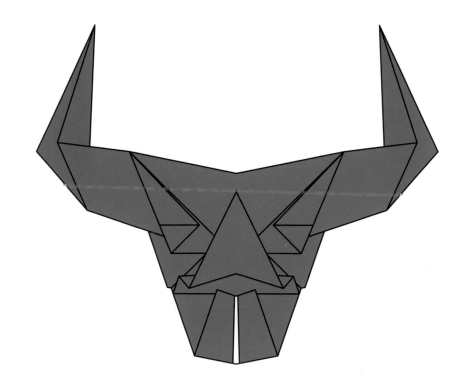

DUCK

You don't see many orange ducks! But, it's a nice color, don't you think?

1 Valley fold a square in half.

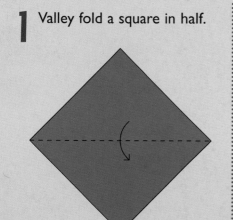

2 Valley fold the top layer upward.

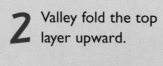

3 Does it look like this? Good! Now valley fold and unfold to crease.

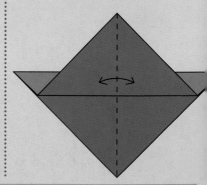

4 Valley fold one side. Line the paper up against the crease.

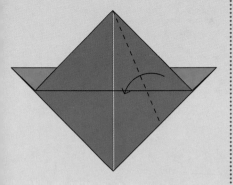

6 Valley fold the left side, like you did before on the right.

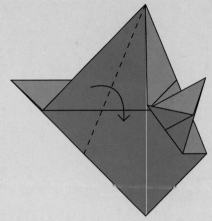

8 Turn the form over.

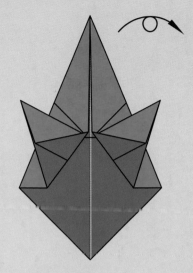

5 Now make a valley fold on the dashed line.

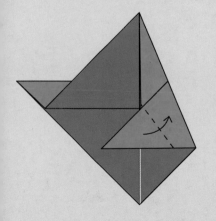

7 And valley fold back again.

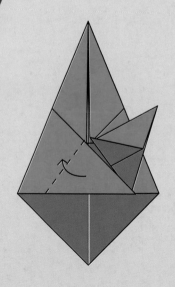

9 Make a small pleat fold near the tip.

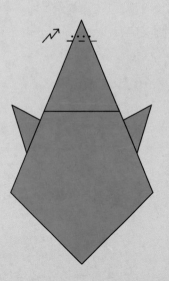

10 Valley fold in half.

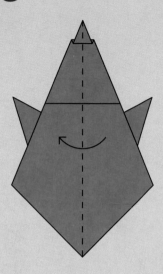

11 Turn the form to the left.

12 Unfold both sides upward as shown.

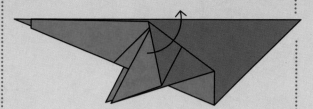

13 Make an outside reverse fold.

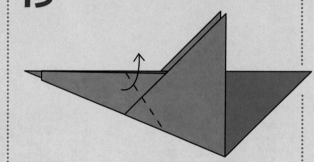

14 Mountain fold the top layer to the inside.

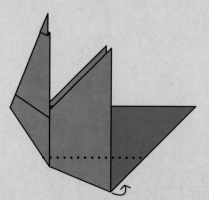

15 Valley fold the next layer.

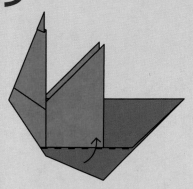

18 Pull the duck's bill into position, and squash fold.

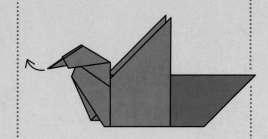

16 Tuck the flap inside.

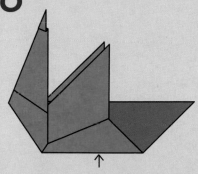

19 Make an inside reverse fold to start the tail.

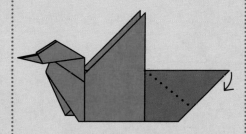

21 Valley fold upward.

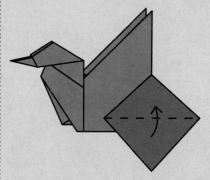

17 Make an outside reverse fold for the neck.

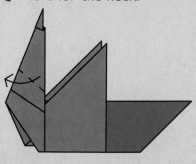

20 Valley fold to the left.

22 Valley fold tail.

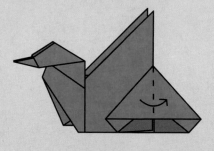

23 Pull the tip outward, and squash fold.

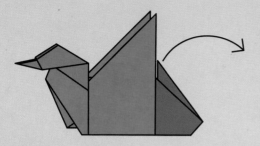

26 ...hide flap inside (see arrow).

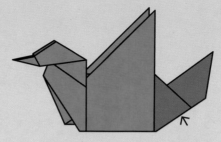

24 Mountain fold top layer to inside.

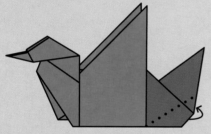

27 Valley fold both wings out to sides.

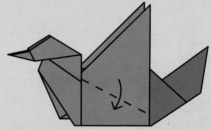

25 Valley fold bottom layer forward, and...

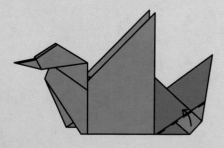

28 You've made a Duck. Ducks like to swim on ponds, too

Jet Fighter

When made out of paper, jet fighters can be any color of the rainbow!

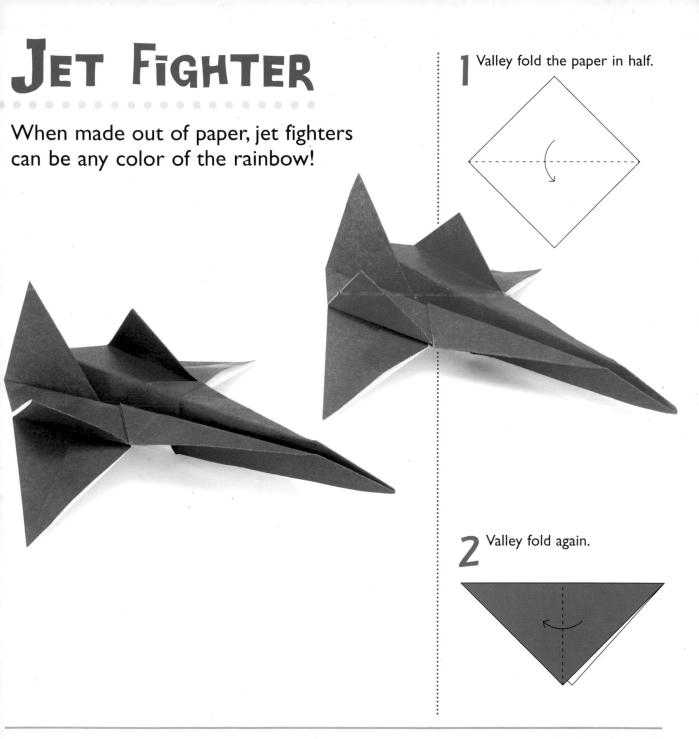

1 Valley fold the paper in half.

2 Valley fold again.

3 Spread apart the top layer and squash it flat on the dotted line.

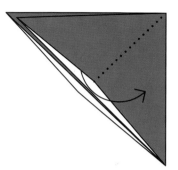

4 Turn the form over.

5 Again, spread apart the top layer and squash it flat on the dotted line.

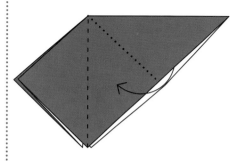

6 Valley fold and unfold the top layer.

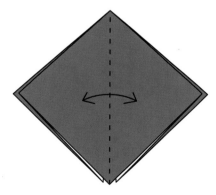

7 Make three valley folds on the dashed lines, then unfold.

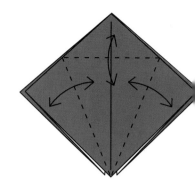

8 Pull top layer as shown and fold on the valley line

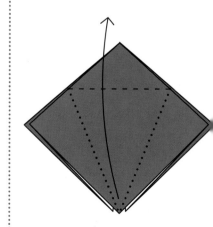

9 This is how it looks when you are doing step 8.

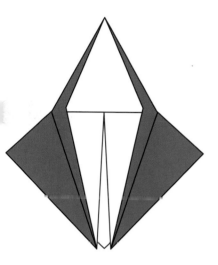

10 When it looks like this, valley fold the two parts on the dashed lines.

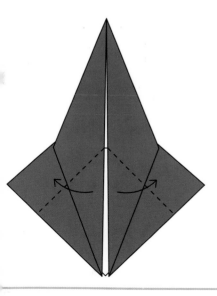

11 Turn the form over.

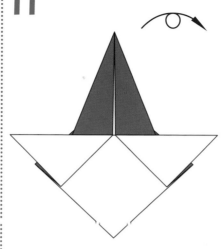

12 Valley fold the triangle in the direction of the arrow.

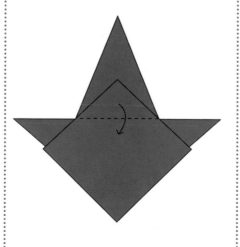

13 Valley fold the form in half.

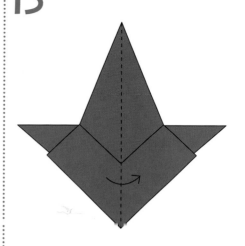

14 Turn the form so the jet is flying to the left.

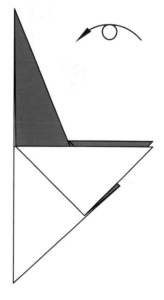

15 Valley fold the top layer downward.

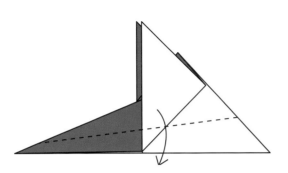

16 Fold the other layer to the back on the dotted line.

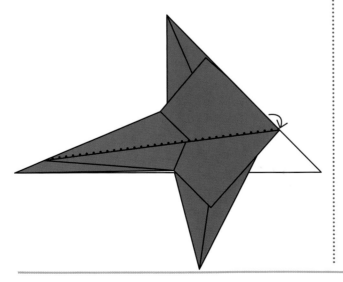

17 Valley fold the top layer upward on the dashed line.

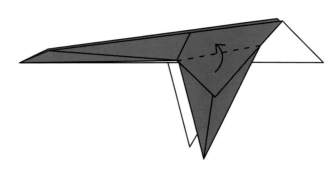

18 Turn the jet over to the other side.

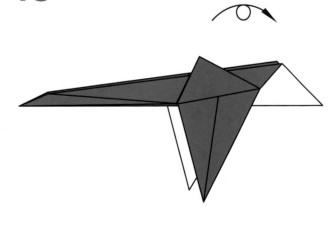

19 Now valley fold the top layer on this side on the dashed line.

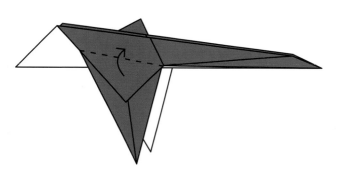

21 Make an inside reverse fold.

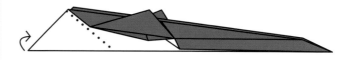

20 Unfold the jet's body out to the sides to balance the wings.

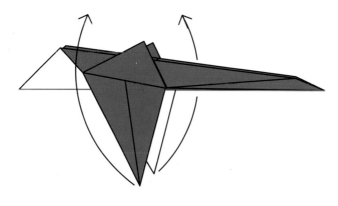

22 Now you can be the pilot of your own Jet Fighter!

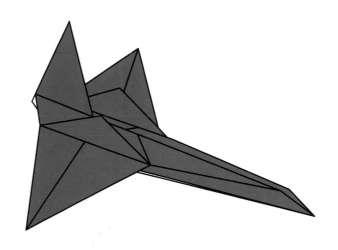

Squaring-Off Paper

Here is an easy way to get square paper for practice and for folding projects.

1 Take any sheet of paper. Valley fold it diagonally to the opposite edge.

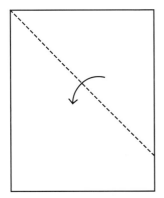

2 Cut the edge of the paper off as shown.

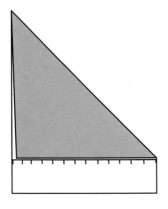

3 Unfold...

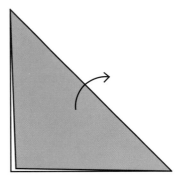

4 ...and the paper is square!

ndex